Informing the legislative debate since 1914

The Berry Amendment: Requiring Defense Procurement to Come from Domestic Sources

Valerie Bailey Grasso
Specialist in Defense Acquisition

February 24, 2014

Congressional Research Service

7-5700

www.crs.gov

RL31236

Summary

This report examines the original intent and purpose of the Berry Amendment and legislative proposals to amend the application of domestic source restrictions, as well as potential options for Congress. In order to protect the U.S. industrial base during periods of adversity and war, Congress passed domestic source restrictions as part of the 1941 Fifth Supplemental Department of Defense (DOD) Appropriations Act. These provisions later became known as the Berry Amendment. The Berry Amendment (Title 10 United States Code [U.S.C.] §2533a, Requirement to Buy Certain Articles from American Sources; Exceptions) contains a number of domestic source restrictions that prohibit DOD from acquiring food, clothing (including military uniforms), fabrics (including ballistic fibers), stainless steel, and hand or measuring tools that are not grown or produced in the United States. The Berry Amendment applies to DOD purchases only.

On January 31, 2014, DOD issued a solicitation designed to conduct market research to assess the marketplace for the availability of American-made shoes fully compliant with the Berry Amendment. According to one February 2014 press report, four firms have told the Defense Logistics Agency that they could produce U.S.-made athletic footwear for military personnel.

H.R. 1960, the House-proposed National Defense Authorization Act (NDAA) for FY2014, was introduced in the House on May 14, passed the House in a recorded vote (315-108) on June 14, and was referred to the Senate on July 8, 2013. The bill contained several provisions which would, if enacted into law, impact domestic source restrictions under the Berry Amendment, including the procurement of American flags, footwear for enlisted service members, contracts for textiles and clothing, and periodic audits by the Inspector General on contracts for goods and services.

S. 1197, the Senate-proposed NDAA for FY2014, was introduced on June 20, 2013, and referred to the Armed Services Committee. Senate Report (S. Rept.) 113-44, which accompanied S. 1197, directed both DOD and the Army to study the status of domestic sourcing for athletic footwear for enlisted members, and to determine if there were sufficient quantities and with the appropriate qualities to meet the needs and requirement of DOD. The committee also directed DOD to submit a report to Congress including any audits or auditing policy, investigations and enforcement, and other requirements relating to DOD's contracting for textiles, clothing, and athletic footwear.

P.L. 113-66, the NDAA for FY2014 (H.R. 3304) was signed into law on December 26, 2013. The Berry Amendment-related provisions proposed in H.R. 1960 and S. 1197 were not entirely incorporated into the enacted bill. A discussion was provided in the legislative text and joint explanation statement which accompanied H.R. 3304.

Some policy makers believe that policies like the Berry Amendment contradict free trade policies, and that the presence and degree of such competition is the most effective tool for promoting efficiencies and improving quality. On the other hand, some other policy makers believe that key domestic sectors (like manufacturing) need the protections afforded by the Berry Amendment. The debate over the Berry Amendment raises several questions, among them (1) If the United States does not produce a solely domestic item, or if U.S. manufacturers are at maximum production capability, should DOD restrict procurement from foreign sources; and (2) to what extent do U.S. national security interests and industrial base concerns justify waiver of the Berry Amendment?

Contents

Contacts

Major Developments

Defense Logistics Agency Issues Formal Notice for American-made Shoes

On January 31, 2014, DOD issued a solicitation designed to conduct market research to assess the availability of American-made shoes fully compliant with the Berry Amendment.[1] The solicitation appeared in Federal Business Opportunities, and stated that there is no current contract for shoes, or a guarantee that a contract is or will be forthcoming. Excerpts of the solicitation follow. Responses to the solicitation were requested by February 18, 2014.

> In order to assess the marketplace, we request interested providers identify all Berry Compliant Athletic (Running) shoes being sold in the commercial marketplace to include: (1) a general description of each item, including the various fits and sizes, (2) the volume of commercial sales for each of those products for the past 1 to 3 years, (3) cost and/or selling price, (4) manufacturing capacity of those items to include any minimum order quantities, economic production quantities as well as monthly and annual maximum production capabilities (5) production lead time and (6) manufacturing location.
>
> For those capable of manufacturing a domestically Compliant Athletic (Running) Shoe but have not yet produced or sold any, please provide, to the extent possible, the information requested above along with any additional actions you would need to take in order to make those products available in the commercial marketplace.
>
> Additionally, please be sure to confirm that your product offering is fully domestic, including all components materials and subcomponent assemblies.[2]

According to one press report, DLA has announced that four companies have reported being capable of producing 100% domestic, U.S.-made, athletic footwear for military personnel.[3]

H.R. 3304, the National Defense Authorization Act for FY2014

P.L. 113-66, the NDAA for FY2014 (H.R. 3304) was signed into law on December 26, 2013. Some of the Berry Amendment-related provisions proposed in H.R. 1960 and S. 1197 were not incorporated into the enacted bill. A discussion was provided in the joint explanation statement which accompanied the bill. Excerpts appear below.[4]

---

[1] 252.225-7012 Preference for Certain Domestic Commodities.

[2] Defense Logistics Agency. Athletic Footwear-Berry Compliant. Solicitation Number SPE1C1, January 31, 2014, at https://www.fbo.gov/?s=opportunity&mode=form&id=c05c58a24e25bc85a16b8ddf7a34c7ec&tab=core&_cview=0. For press reports, see "Only in the USA: Lawmakers push for American-made, military-issue sneakers for recruits. *Air Force Times*, February 17, 2014. Accessed online at http://www.airforcetimes.com/article/20140218/NEWS07/302180021/Lawmakers-push-American-made-military-issue-sneakers.

[3] Wright, Austin. Four Firms Answer DOD Call For U.S.-Made Sneakers. *Politico Pro* online, February 24, 2014. According to the article, Stacey Hajdak from DLA Troop Support spoke on behalf of DLA. CRS attempted to contact DLA on February 21, 2014 but did not receive a response.

[4] P.L. 113-66 was signed into law on December 26, 2013. See Legislative Text and Joint Explanatory Statement to accompany H.R. 3304 (Committee Print).

Compliance with domestic source requirements for footwear furnished to enlisted members of the Armed Forces upon their initial entry into the Armed Forces

The House bill contained a provision (Section 839) that would amend section 418 of title 37, United States Code, by requiring the Department of Defense to issue athletic footwear compliant with the requirement detailed in section 2533a of title 10, United States Code, to members of the Armed Forces upon their initial entry in lieu of a cash allowance.

The Senate committee reported bill contained no similar provision.

The agreement does not contain the provision.

We note that Congress passed the Berry Amendment in 1941 to ensure that American soldiers train and operate, to the greatest extent practicable, in American-made materials. The Berry Amendment specifically covers footwear listed in Federal Supply Class 8430 or 8435.

The Army, in 2001, and the Air Force, in 2008, have moved away from issuing athletic footwear to new recruits. Instead, new recruits are given an allowance to acquire athletic footwear from the service exchange.

During this period of time, no athletic footwear was available that could have met the requirements of the Berry Amendment without a waiver. It has been reported that at least one domestic contractor is now producing such footwear.

Therefore, we direct the Under Secretary of Defense for Acquisition, Technology and Logistics to issue a Sources Sought to determine whether there are any domestic manufacturers of Berry Amendment compliant athletic footwear that meets the Department's requirements.

We further direct that any responses to the Sources Sought be evaluated by the Defense Logistics Agency and an independent entity to determine whether (1) such offered athletic footwear meets the requirements of the Berry Amendment and (2) whether Department requirements are actually met. Such review should consider the various sizes and fits of athletic shoes offered, cost, and capacity of suppliers to meet military requirements.[5]

Periodic audits of contracting compliance by the Inspector General of the Department of Defense (Section 1601)

The House bill contained a provision (Section 1601) that would require the Inspector General of the Department of Defense to conduct an audit of the Department's compliance with contracting

practices and policies related to procurement under section 2533a of title 10, United States Code, which pertains to the requirement to buy certain articles from American sources and is frequently referred to as the "Berry Amendment." This section would also require the Inspector General to include the findings of such periodic audits as part of the semiannual report transmitted to congressional committees as required by the Inspector General Act of 1978 (P.L. 95-452).

The Senate committee-reported bill contained no similar provision.

---

[5] P.L. 113-66. See Legislative Text and Joint Explanatory Statement accompanying H.R. 3304 (Committee Print.), pages 607-608.

The agreement contains the provision with a clarifying amendment.[6]

See the following excerpt from H.R. 3304.

Section 1601. Periodic Audits of Contracting Compliance by Inspector General of the Department of Defense

> (a) Requirement for Periodic Audits of Contracting Compliance-The Inspector General of the Department of Defense shall conduct periodic audits of contracting practices and policies related to procurement under section 2533a of title 10, United States Code.
>
> (b) Requirement for Additional Information in Semiannual Reports-The Inspector General of the Department of Defense shall ensure that findings and other information resulting from audits conducted pursuant to subsection (a) are included in the semiannual report transmitted to congressional committees under section 8(f)(1) of the Inspector General Act of 1978 (5 U.S.C. App.).[7]

H.R. 1960, the House-proposed National Defense Authorization Act for Fiscal Year 2014

H.R. 1960 was introduced in the House on May 14, passed the House in a recorded vote (315-108) on June 14, and was referred to the Senate on July 8, 2013. The bill contained several provisions which would, if enacted into law, impact domestic source restrictions.

- Section 817 would have amended 10 U.S.C. 2533b by requiring the procurement of American flags to come from domestic sources;[8]

- Section 833 would have required DOD to report to Congress, within 180 days of enactment of the act, on supply chain vulnerabilities during sole source procurement. The report would include a list of the components in the DOD supply chain for which one supplier controls over 50% of the global market, a list of supply chain parts where there is inadequate information to determine whether there is a single source for components, as well as the Secretary of Defense's recommendations on which single source suppliers create vulnerabilities and recommendations on how to reduce them;

- Section 839 would have required DOD to meet domestic sourcing requirements for footwear issued to enlisted members, provided that DOD can certify that there are at least two domestic manufacturers of footwear that can meet the requirements of the Berry Amendment;[9]

- Section 1601 would have required the DOD Inspector General to conduct periodic audits of contracting practices and policies related to the Berry Amendment. These audits shall be conducted at least once every three years; and

- H.Rept. 113-102 (which accompanied H.R. 1960) contained two "Items of Special Interest" that reflected the Committee's interest and concern over the

---

[6] Ibid., p. 698.

[7] H.R. 3304, Subtitle A. Defense Industrial Base Matters.

[8] For further information, see "Department of Defense's Procurement of American Flags."

[9] H.R. 2188 (§839) was introduced on May 23, 2013 and referred to the House Armed Services Committee. A companion bill, S. 1051, was introduced on the same day and referred to the Senate Armed Services Committee.

enforcement of domestic source provisions under the Berry Amendment, as described here.

Contracting for Textiles and Clothing

The committee supports maintaining the integrity of section 2533a of title 10, United States Code, commonly referred to as the 'Berry Amendment,' which requires 100% U.S. content for certain products sourced for the Armed Forces. The committee is concerned with protecting the supply chain and domestic production base for components and weapon systems that are vital to the Armed Forces. In addition, the practice of sourcing certain products and materials from foreign entities in violation of the Berry Amendment may harm the domestic industrial base, as well as result in U.S. job losses. Therefore, elsewhere in this Act, the committee includes a provision that would require the Inspector General of the Department of Defense to periodically review the Department's compliance with established restrictions.[10]

Periodic Audits of Contracting Compliance by the Inspector General of the Department of Defense

This section would require the Inspector General of the Department of Defense to conduct an audit of the Department's compliance with contracting practices and policies related to procurement under section 2533a of title 10, United States Code, which pertains to the requirement to buy certain articles from American sources and is frequently referred to as the 'Berry Amendment.' This section would also require the Inspector General to include the findings of such periodic audits as part of the semiannual report transmitted to congressional committees as required by the Inspector General Act of 1978 (P.L. 95-452).[11]

S. 1197, the Senate-proposed National Defense Authorization Act for FY2014

S. 1197 was introduced on June 20, 2013, and referred to the Armed Services Committee. S.Rept. 113-44, which accompanied S. 1197, directed both DOD and the Army to study the status of domestic sourcing for athletic footwear for enlisted members, as discussed here.

Therefore, the committee directs U.S. Army Natick Soldier Research, Development, and Engineering Center to undergo a study, to be completed no later than January 1, 2014, of currently available Berry compliant athletic footwear to ascertain whether the Department's needs could be satisfied for new recruits. The committee believes this study should review the various sizes and fit of athletic shoes required the cost and capacity of products available in sufficient quantity and quality to meet the needs of the Department of Defense (DOD), and whether such footwear could be made.

During roughly the last decade, certain procurement incidents and policy changes have created some level of unease with respect to the Berry Amendment's application to not only athletic footwear but also textiles and clothing. As such, the committee directs DOD to submit a publicly releasable report to the congressional defense committees that includes, but not be limited to, any audits or auditing policy, investigations and enforcement, incentives, procurement officer training, and regulatory interpretation guidelines relating to the Department's contracting for textiles and clothing contained in

---

[10] H.Rept. 113-102, Title XVI. Industrial Base Matters, Items of Special Interest.

[11] §1601, H.R. 1960.

Federal Supply Codes 83 and 84, and athletic footwear listed in Federal Supply Class 8430 and 8435.[12]

Department of Defense's Procurement of American Flags

In light of the public debate raised concerning the announcement that U.S. Olympic uniforms were procured from foreign sources, some questions have been raised concerning DOD's procurement of American flags. CRS contacted officials from the Defense Logistics Agency and asked the following questions. DLA officials provided answers to those specific questions, as provided below.[13]

1. From what sources does DOD procure American flags?

   DOD procures flags through DLA Troop Support. DLA Troop Support does not purchase flags that are not made in the U.S.

2. Is the procurement of U.S. flags under the authority of the Berry Amendment? Why or why not?

   U.S. flags are not specifically included in the Berry Amendment, but the fabric used to manufacture flags is covered under Title 10, USC §2533a (b) (1) (D). Although the Berry Amendment does not apply to purchases of Berry-covered items under $150,000 [10 USC §2533a (h)], the Buy American Act does apply.

3. Are U.S. flags specifically exempted from the Berry Amendment?

   No. U.S. flags are not specifically exempted from the Berry Amendment. However, it should be noted that only items specifically listed in the Berry Amendment are covered [10 USC §2533a (b)], so an item does not have to be specifically exempted in order not to be covered by the Berry Amendment. As noted in response to question 2, the fabric used in flags is covered by the Berry Amendment. The Berry Amendment coverage of rayon used in flags and other military clothing and textile items was waived in 2001 by the Under Secretary of Defense (Acquisition, Technology and Logistics) by means of a domestic non-availability determination (DNAD) based on a determination that it is domestically unavailable. This determination was made pursuant to a Berry Amendment provision authorizing waiver of its coverage based on domestic non-availability of a covered item (10 USC §2533a(c)). Market research was conducted as recently as 2011, which confirmed that rayon yarn/thread is still not available domestically.

4. Does the Department of Defense have contracts with domestic suppliers of U.S. flags? Is there a list of the domestic flag producers?

   Yes. DLA has several Long Term Contracts (LTC) and has also made multiple small purchases, all with domestic suppliers. There is no list of domestic flag producers. DLA currently contracts with the following vendors: Allied Materials, Kansas City, MO; Alphasoft/Dawn's Early Light, Bellevue, WA; US Flag & Signal, Portsmouth, VA; Valley Forge Flag Company, Wyomissing, PA, and All Seasons, Post Falls, ID.

5. If the Department of Defense is purchasing U.S. flags from U.S. companies, are they using non-U.S. sourced materials for the flags? If so, what materials, countries of origin, and in what quantities (fiscal year)?

---

[12] Subtitle D, Items of Special Interest, Application of the Berry Amendment to the Acquisition of Athletic Footwear in the Department of Defense.

[13] The following information was provided to CRS, from DLA officials, on July 19, 2012.

As noted in response to question 3, rayon is not domestically available. If the flag specification calls for a rayon component, rayon is covered under the 2001 DNAD referred to an answer to question 3 above. We are not aware of the countries of origin for rayon.[14]

Other Legislative Provisions

Legislation Enacted

- Section 826 of H.R. 4310, the NDAA for FY2013, contains a provision requiring textile components supplied by DOD for uniforms for the Afghanistan National Army or the Afghanistan National Police is procured in accordance with the Berry Amendment, and that no exceptions or exemptions under 10 U.S.C. 2533a shall apply.[15]

- P.L. 112-81, the NDAA for FY2012 (H.R. 1540) contained a provision (§368) which required that "best value" be the basis of awards for contracts for tents and other temporary structures regardless of where purchased, by DOD,[16] or by another agency on behalf of DOD, as well as another provision (§821) which clarified the intent of the Berry Amendment when applied to the purchase of tents, tarpaulins, or covers from domestic sources.[17] On June 29, 2012, DOD published an interim rule to implement Sections 368 and 821 of the NDAA for FY2012. The public is invited to submitted comments by August 28, 2012.[18]

- P.L. 112-81 also contained a provision (§822) that repealed the sunset of the authority to procure fire resistant rayon fiber, from foreign sources, used for the production of uniforms.

- P.L. 111-383, the Ike Skelton National Defense Authorization Act for FY2011, adopted the final rule (to implement §821) which prohibited DOD from specifying the use of fire-resistant, rayon fiber in solicitations issued before January 1, 2015. Section 821 also required the Comptroller General to submit reports to the House and Senate Armed Services Committees, not later than March 15, 2011, that assessed the supply chain for the procurement of fire-resistant and fire-retardant fibers and materials for the production of military uniforms.[19] The House Armed Services Committee expressed its concern over DOD's application of the Berry Amendment to tents, tarpaulins, or covers, as

---

[14] For more information, see DOD's Defense Procurement and Acquisition Policy's website at http://www.acq.osd mil/dpap/cpic/ic/domestic_non-availability_determinations_dnads html. Also, see GAO 11-682R, Military Uniforms: Issues Related to the Supply of Flame Resistant Fibers for the Production of Military Uniforms, June 30, 2011, 40 p. Accessed online at http://www.gao.gov/products/GAO-11-682R.

[15] P.L. 112-239 (H.R. 4310) was signed into law on January 2, 2013.

[16] §368 reads: "In determining the best value to the United States under this section, the Secretary shall consider the total life-cycle costs of such tents or structures, including the costs associated with any equipment or fuel needed to heat or cool such tents or structures."

[17] §2533a (b) (1) (C) of Title 10, U.S.C., is amended by inserting "and the structural components thereof" after the word "tents."

[18] Defense Federal Acquisition Regulation Supplement: Acquisition of Tents and Other Temporary Structures (DFARS Case 2012-D015). *Federal Register*, Vol. 77, No. 126, June 29, 2012, pages 38734-38736. Accessed online at http://www.gpo.gov/fdsys/pkg/FR-2012-06-29/pdf/2012-15563.pdf.

[19] GAO 11-682R, Military Uniforms: Issues Related to the Supply of Flame Resistant Fibers for the Production of Military Uniforms, June 30, 2011, 40 p. Accessed online at http://www.gao.gov/products/GAO-11-682R.

---

reflected in H.Rept. 111-419 for H.R. 5136 (the proposed NDAA for FY2011), as quoted here.[20]

APPLICATION OF BERRY AMENDMENT TO TENTS AND RELATED ITEMS

The committee is aware that the Director, Defense Logistics Agency has chosen to interpret the requirement to buy certain articles from domestic sources per subsection (b) of section 2533a of title 10, United States Code, in such a manner that it applies expressly to tents, tarpaulins, or covers, but not to the materials and components of tents, tarpaulins, or covers. The committee is concerned that this narrow interpretation of the statute is inconsistent with the law. Therefore, the committee directs the Director, Defense Logistics Agency to review the interpretation of the current statute to ensure that it is compliant with both the law and with congressional intent and submit a report to the congressional defense committees not later than October 1, 2011, explaining how the committees' concerns were addressed.[21]

- P.L. 111-383, the Ike Skelton National Defense Authorization Act for FY2011 (§847), provided a non-availability exception for the procurement of domestic hand or measuring tools. On March 17, 2011, DOD issued an interim rule in accordance with Section 847. The interim rule was published in the *Federal Register* and the public comment period extended through May 16, 2011. The final rule was published on August 19, 2011.[22]

GAO Reports on the Berry Amendment

A June 2011 GAO report examined the use of fire-resistant and fire-retardant materials in military uniforms. Military uniforms are procured in accordance with the provisions of the Federal Acquisition Regulation (FAR), DLA's own internal regulations, the Berry Amendment, and the Buy American Act (BAA).[23] Legislative initiatives which may impact the procurement of military uniforms were enacted in P.L. 111-383 (H.R. 6523), the Ike Skelton National Defense Authorization Act for FY2011. Specifically, Section 821 of P.L. 111-383 required the Comptroller General to submit reports to the House and Senate Armed Services Committees, not later than March 15, 2011, that assessed the supply chain for the procurement of fire-resistant and fire-retardant fibers and materials for the production of military uniforms. This legislation reflected congressional concern that with the continued threat of improvised explosive device (IED) attacks, all combat personnel were subject to the possibility of fire-related injuries. Thus vehicle and aircraft fires remained a significant force protection and safety threat, whether they occurred during ongoing combat operations or training for future deployment.

GAO was directed to provide an assessment of the following areas:

---

[20] H.R. 5136 was introduced in the House on April 26, 2010, and referred to the Senate on June 28, 2010. A related bill, H.R. 6523, was introduced in the House on December 15, 2010, passed the House on December 17, 2010, passed the Senate on December 22, 2010, and signed by the President on January 7, 2011, as P.L. 111-383.

[21] H.Rept. 111-491 for the National Defense Authorization Act for FY2011 (H.R. 5136).

[22] Defense Federal Acquisition Regulation Supplement; Non-availability Exception for Procurement of Hand or Measuring Tools. (DFARS Case 2011-D025), Federal Register, March 17, 2011 (Volume 76, Number 52).

[23] The Buy American Act (41 U.S.C. 10a through 10d, as amended) is the principal domestic preference statute governing most procurement by the federal government. It restricts foreign access to U.S. government procurement by giving preference to domestically produced, manufactured, or home-grown products. For further discussion of the Buy American Act, refer to CRS Report 97-765, *The Buy American Act: Requiring Government Procurements to Come from Domestic Sources*, by John R. Luckey.

(A) The current and anticipated sources of fire-resistant rayon fiber for the production of military uniforms;

(B) The extent to which fire-resistant rayon fiber has unique properties that provide advantages for the production of military uniforms;

(C) The extent to which the efficient procurement of fire-resistant rayon fiber for the production of military uniforms is impeded by existing statutory or regulatory requirements;

(D) The actions the Department of Defense has taken to identify alternatives to fire-resistant rayon fiber for the production of military uniforms;

(E) The extent to which such alternatives provide an adequate substitute for fire-resistant rayon fiber for the production of military uniforms;

(F) The impediments to the use of such alternatives, and the actions the Department has taken to overcome such impediments;

(G) The extent to which uncertainty regarding the future availability of fire-resistant rayon fiber results in instability or inefficiency for elements of the United States textile industry that use fire-resistant rayon fiber, and the extent to which that instability or inefficiency results in less efficient business practices, impedes investment and innovation, and thereby results or may result in higher costs, delayed delivery, or a lower quality of product delivered to the Government; and

(H) The extent to which any modifications to existing law or regulation may be necessary to ensure the efficient acquisition of fire-resistant fiber or alternative fire-resistant products for the production of military uniforms.[24]

GAO found that an Austrian company was the sole source for fire-resistant rayon fiber for the manufacture of fire-resistant uniforms for military personnel, that DOD had taken steps to identify and test alternative fire-resistant, fabric blends to meet current demands, and that there was debate over whether fire-resistant rayon's flame resistant characteristics posed a superior advantage over other alternatives. GAO did not provide a recommendation.[25]

GAO was also congressionally directed to assess whether the Berry Amendment was sufficient protection for the defense industrial base and whether alternatives and solutions existed to keep critical industries healthy and viable, in times of both war and peace. This 2003 report required GAO to determine whether the Defense Logistics Agency (DLA) was properly implementing applicable statutory and regulatory guidance for "best value" purchases and to solicit DLA views on the domestic clothing and textile supplier base. GAO officials acknowledged that the Berry Amendment was a positive factor in helping DOD to maintain a domestic supplier for some of DOD's unique military needs; however, officials pointed out that the overall domestic clothing and textile industry was in decline due to declining employment and production levels, as well as the implementation of various free trade agreements that may affect different levels of the domestic supply chain.[26]

---

[24] §821 of P.L. 111-383, the Ike Skelton National Defense Authorization Act for FY2011. The bill was signed into law on January 7, 2011.

[25] U.S. Government Accountability Office. Military Uniforms: Issues Related to the Supply of Flame Resistant Fibers for the Production of Military uniforms. GAO-11-682R, June 2011. The report can be accessed online at http://www.gao.gov/new.items/d11682r.pdf.

[26] Contract Management: DLA Properly Implemented Best Value Contracting for Clothing and Textiles and Views the Supplier Base as Uncertain. Report to the chairman and ranking Minority Member, Committee on Armed Services, House of Representatives. U.S. General Accounting Office, GAO-03-440, February 2003. 18 p.

The Berry Amendment and DHS

One legislative provision was enacted and three other provisions were proposed that would impact the application of the Berry Amendment to DHS.

Legislation Enacted

- P.L. 111-5, the American Reinvestment and Recovery Act of 2009 (H.R. 1), contained a provision (§604) that was similar to the Berry Amendment. Section 604 affected all funds appropriated or otherwise made available to DHS. These restrictions prohibited DHS from the purchase of certain textiles unless the items are grown, reprocessed, reused, or produced in the United States. Section 604 is also referred to as the "Kissell Amendment."[27]

Legislation Proposed

- S. 2114 (112th Congress), the Berry Amendment Extension Act, was introduced on February 15, 2012, and referred to the Senate Homeland Security Committee and Governmental Affairs. The proposed measure would prohibit the Department of Homeland Security from procuring certain items directly related to national security unless the items are grown, reprocessed, reused, or produced in the United States.

- H.R. 679 (112th Congress), the Berry Amendment Extension Act, was introduced on February 11, 2011, and on February 17, 2011, was referred to the House Homeland Security Subcommittee on Oversight, Investigations, and Management. The proposed measure would amend Subtitle H of Title VIII of the Homeland Security Act of 2002 to prohibit DHS from the purchase of clothing, tents, tarpaulins, and certain other textiles unless the items are grown, reprocessed, reused, or produced in the United States.

- H.R. 3116 (111th Congress), the Berry Amendment Extension Act, was introduced on July 7, 2009, by Representative Larry Kissell. The proposed measure would have prohibited the purchase of clothing, tents, tarpaulins, and certain other textiles unless the items are grown, reprocessed, reused, or produced in the United States. The bill was referred to the Senate Homeland Security and Governmental Affairs Committee. No further action was taken.

- H.R. 917 (110th Congress), the Berry Amendment Extension Act, was introduced on February 8, 2007, by Representative Robin Hayes. The proposed measure would have prohibited DHS from the purchase of clothing, tents, tarpaulins, and certain other textiles unless the items are grown, reprocessed, reused, or produced in the United States. The bill was referred to the House Homeland Security

---

[27] This bill contains restrictions on the Department of Homeland Security's (DHS) acquisition of certain foreign textile products. Specifically, §604 of the American Reinvestment and Recovery Act, codified as 6 U.S.C. 453b, limits DHS acquisition of foreign textile products under DHS contract actions entered into on or after August 16, 2009, using funds appropriated or otherwise made available to DHS on or before February 17, 2009, the date of the act. DHS may not use those funds for the procurement of certain clothing and other textile items directly related to the national security interests of the United States if such items are not domestically grown, reprocessed, reused, or produced in the United States. See Revision of Department of Homeland Security Acquisition Regulation: Restrictions on Foreign Acquisition (HSAR Case 2009-004). http://www.federalregister.gov/articles/2010/06/09/2010-13804/revision-of-department-of-homeland-security-acquisition-regulation-restrictions-on-foreign#p-12.

Subcommittee on Managements, Investigations, and Oversight. No further action was taken.

In 2008 there were first media reports that the Under Secretary of Defense for Acquisition, Technology, and Logistics had considered several legislative proposals to broaden the exceptions provided under the Berry Amendment. *Inside the Pentagon* reported that John Young, then DOD's senior acquisition executive, had formally submitted proposals to be considered as part of DOD's submission for the FY2009 National Defense Authorization bill. One such proposal would have granted DOD authority to waive the requirements of the Berry Amendment during so-called emergency operations. Such emergency operations might include military action taken against U.S. adversaries, military action in response to an attack with weapons of mass destruction, or military action resulting from national emergencies declared by the President. Another proposal would have authorized military procurement officials to give contracting preference to indigenous groups for the purpose of expanding economic development in a contingency operation.[28] DOD had also submitted a legislative proposal that would have amended the Berry Amendment to permit the purchase of fresh fruits and vegetables from all sources.[29]

Berry Amendment Resources

Two public resources provide answers to many of the most often-asked questions on the Berry Amendment. DOD's Office of Defense Procurement and Acquisition Policy (DPAP) has prepared a "Frequently Asked Questions" compendium of general information on the Berry Amendment. The questions and answers ranged from origin and history, authority, policy, and exceptions; comparisons with other domestic source restrictions like the Buy American Act; the policy governing determinations of non-availability (DNAD); and many questions often raised by suppliers and other industry personnel.[30]

Also, the U.S. Department of Commerce has launched a website to provide textile and other manufacturers a resource for the latest information on the Berry Amendment. According to the website, this resource was compiled with the support of the Commerce's International Trade Administration's Office of Textiles and Apparel, DOD, Office of the Under Secretary of Defense for Acquisition, Technology, and Logistics, and DPAP; Army, Air Force, and Navy acquisition offices.[31]

Background

The Berry Amendment contains a number of domestic source restrictions that prohibit DOD from acquiring food, clothing, fabrics (including ballistic fibers), specialty metals, stainless steel, and hand or measuring tools that are not grown or produced in the United States.[32]

---

[28] Young Seeks Legislative Changes to Streamline Contingency Buying. *Inside the Pentagon*, February 28, 2008, Vol. 24, No. 9.

[29] U.S. Department of Defense. Seventh Package of Legislative Proposals Sent to Congress for Inclusion in the National Defense Authorization Act for FY2009, sent to Congress on May 28, 2008. See http://www.dod mil/dodgc/olc/legispro html.

[30] The Defense Contract Management Agency has provided a list of items for which waivers have been issued due to lack of a domestic supplier, as well as the corrective action plans submitted by suppliers to meet compliance with the Berry Amendment. For further information, see http://www.acq.osd mil/dpap/cpic/ic/berry_amendment_faq html.

[31] http://web.ita.doc.gov/tacgi/eamain nsf/BerryAmendment/Berry%20Amendment?Opendocument.

[32] 10 U.S.C. §2533a, Requirement to Buy Certain Articles from American Sources; Exceptions.

Congress and DOD have long debated the need to protect the U.S. defense industrial base by restricting certain federal procurement to U.S. markets through legislation known as "domestic source restrictions."[33] Many defense appropriations bills passed since 1942 have included some mention of a preference for U.S. articles, supplies, and materials. One particular group of domestic source restrictions was first enacted into law on April 5, 1941, as part of the FY1941 Fifth Supplemental National Defense Appropriations Act, P.L. 77-29. During the second session of the 82nd Congress, Elias Y. Berry, Representative from South Dakota, introduced two bills to amend the Buy America Act to include wool as a product or material, produced or manufactured in the United States.[34] Reportedly, this amendment would come to be known as the Berry Amendment.

On December 13, 2001, the passage of the FY2002 National Defense Authorization Act codified and modified the Berry Amendment,[35] making it a permanent part of the United States Code. Under the Berry Amendment, the Secretary of Defense has the authority to waive the requirement to buy domestically, under certain conditions.[36]

The 2001 controversy over the procurement of black berets and the waiver authority of the Secretary of Defense, as well as the presence of other domestic source provisions, have created considerable interest in the Berry Amendment. Some policy makers believe that the Berry Amendment's restrictions (like the specialty metal clause) contradict free trade policies, and that the presence and degree of such competition is the most effective tool for promoting efficiencies and improving quality. Others believe that U.S.-based companies need the protections afforded by the Berry Amendment. These two views have been the subject of ongoing debate in Congress.

Controversy over the Berry Amendment

On October 17, 2000, the Army Chief of Staff, General Eric Shinseki, announced that the black beret would become the standard headgear for the U.S. Army. The Army planned to issue a one-piece beret to each of the 1.3 million active duty and reserve soldiers during the spring of 2001, while a second beret would be issued to each soldier in the fall of 2001. The Army was to pay approximately $23.8 million for about 4.7 million berets. DOD awarded the first contract to Bancroft, an Arkansas-based company that had manufactured military headgear since World War I. Other contracts were awarded to several foreign manufacturing firms; five of the foreign firms had production facilities in the People's Republic of China, Romania, Sri Lanka, and other low-wage countries.

---

[33] For a discussion of domestic source restrictions, see "*Defense Acquisition: Rationale for Imposing Domestic Source Restrictions.*" GAO/NSIAD-98-191, July 17, 1998, 20 pages.

[34] Congressional Record. Proceedings and Debates of the 82nd Congress, Second Session. Volume 98-Part 3. March 25, 1952 - April 22, 1952 (pages 3859-3861).

[35] Within DOD regulations, the Berry Amendment can be found in the Defense Federal Acquisition Regulation Supplement (DFARS), Restrictions on Food, Clothing, Fabrics, Specialty Metals, and Hand or Measuring Tools. See DFARS, Part 225.7002.

[36] 10 U.S.C. §2533(c)(d)(e)(f)(g)(h) Exceptions to the Berry Amendment are: when the Secretary of Defense or the Secretary of the military department determine that satisfactory quality and sufficient quantity of any such article or item or specialty metal cannot be procured as and when needed at United States market prices; procurement outside the United States in support of combat operations; procurement by vessels in foreign waters; emergency procurement of perishable foods by an establishment located outside the United States, for the personnel attached to such an establishment; procurement of specialty metals or chemical warfare protective clothing produced outside the United States, under certain circumstances; procurement which complies with reciprocal agreements with foreign governments; procurement of certain foods; procurement for resale at commissaries, exchanges, and other non-appropriated fund instrumentalities; procurement values that are under the simplified acquisition threshold.

To purchase the black berets, the Defense Logistics Agency (DLA)[37] granted two waivers of specific restrictions in the Berry Amendment. The first waiver was granted to DOD so that the department could purchase military uniforms from foreign sources. DLA granted this waiver when it determined that no U.S. firm could produce a sufficient quantity of one-piece, black berets by the Army's deadline. As a result, there were protests from some segments of domestic manufacturing, military and veterans groups, Members of Congress, and the public. The House Small Business Committee held a hearing on May 2, 2001, to discuss the statutory authority to waive Berry Amendment restrictions, as well as the concerns of the small business community regarding the contract award process.

DLA granted the second waiver to allow Bancroft to retain its contract and continue to produce the black berets for the Army, even though Bancroft used materials from foreign sources. Bancroft, the sole U.S. manufacturer of the one-piece beret, had procured materials from two overseas suppliers, who, in turn, had procured material from other foreign sources. Bancroft's president reported that, as early as 1976, DOD had been notified that some beret materials were procured from foreign sources.

On October 4, 2002, DOD announced that the Bancroft Cap Company of Cabot, AR, was awarded a $14.8 million dollar firm-fixed-price contract to manufacture up to 3.6 million black, wool berets for the United States Army and the United States Air Force. The contract was a two-year contract with three one-year options. There were 154 proposals solicited, and 13 vendors responded. The contract was administered through the Defense Supply Center, Philadelphia, PA.[38]

By some, where DOD purchases its berets is viewed as a relatively minor matter, when compared to where it purchases its electronics; specialty metals; and other hardware used for logistics support, communications, and weapons modernization. However, to others small businesses' loss of such a contract to foreign sources can be seen as unacceptable.

History of the Berry Amendment

When Was It Enacted and Why?

The Berry Amendment, which dates from the eve of World War II, was established for a narrowly defined purpose: to ensure that U.S. troops wore military uniforms wholly produced within the United States and to ensure that U.S. troops were fed with food products solely produced in the United States.[39] Other industries, such as tools and specialty metals, were added later. Originally enacted on the eve of World War II, it overrode exceptions added to the Buy American Act of 1933[40] for products procured by the Department of Defense.

---

[37] The Defense Logistics Agency is a logistics combat support agency whose primary role is to provide supplies and services to American military forces worldwide. See http://www.dla.mil.

[38] *Defense Link*. U.S. Department of Defense. Contracts for October 4, 2002.

[39] On April 5, 1941, the Berry Amendment was first enacted as part of the FY1941 Fifth Supplemental National Defense Appropriations Act, P.L. 77-29, 10 U.S.C. §2241 note. The Berry Amendment was made permanent when P.L. 102-396, §9005, was amended by P.L. 103-139, §8005. Since then, Congress has regularly added or subtracted Berry Amendment provisions. On December 13, 2001, the FY2002 National Defense Authorization Act codified and modified the Berry Amendment, repealing Sections 9005 and 8109 of the above-mentioned bills. The Berry Amendment is now codified at 10 U.S.C. 2533a.

[40] See discussion on the Buy American Act, in this report.

In 1941, House and Senate Members held spirited discussions[41] over the passage of what has come to be known as the Berry Amendment, although the precise identity of the author of the amendment remains unknown.[42] Several issues were raised during the debate. Even though the United States was not at war, Congress was concerned that the nation be prepared for adversity and thus provided the impetus for such legislation. Some policy makers were also concerned that despite the enactment of the Buy American Act in 1933, one department of the federal government had reportedly purchased meat from Argentina. Likewise, another department had reportedly contracted to purchase a large quantity of wool, about 50% of which came from foreign sources. Questions were raised over the disposal of some 500 million bushels of surplus wheat, with one policy maker noting that "wheat products and wheat should be purchased from the production here in the United States when we have such a surplus on hand and that our own farmers should be given preference."[43] In an expression of that concern, the original version of the House bill added a provision which required the purchase of American agricultural products in fulfilling national defense needs. (The Senate version initially deleted the provision, but later reinstated it, broadening the bill to include all agriculture.) The bill was enacted into law on April 5, 1941.

Largely as a result of the controversy surrounding the procurement of the black berets, Representative Walter B. Jones introduced a bill to amend Title 10 of the United States Code, thus making the Berry Amendment a permanent provision of law. On April 3, 2001, Representative Jones introduced H.R. 1352 (107th Congress), the purpose of which was to codify and modify the provisions of the Berry Amendment. At the introduction of the bill, Representative Jones stated that the black beret controversy and the decision of the Defense Logistics Agency to waive the Berry Amendment provisions and allow the procurement of berets from foreign sources highlighted the need to review the current law and look for ways to improve the effectiveness of the law. H.R. 1352 would also add a requirement that the Secretary of Defense notify the House and Senate committees on Appropriations, Armed Services, and Small Business before a waiver is made. The provisions of H.R. 1352 were enacted into law as part of the FY2002 National Defense Authorization Act, P.L. 107-107.

How Does the Buy American Act Differ from the Berry Amendment?

The Buy American Act (BAA) and the Berry Amendment are often confused, and the terms are sometimes used interchangeably. The BAA, enacted in 1933, is the principal domestic preference statute governing most procurement by the federal government, while the Berry Amendment, enacted on the eve of World War II, governs DOD procurement only.[44] The BAA seeks to protect

---

[41] An example of a discussion of the issues surrounding the passage of the Berry Amendment can be found in the *Congressional Record*, vol. 87, part 15. 77th Congress, 1st Session, pp. 2460-2984 and pp. 2711-2720.

[42] Legislative reference specialists suggest (but are not certain) that the amendment may have been named after George Leonard Berry (D-TN), who was appointed to serve the remainder of an unexpired U.S. Senate term (1937-38) due to the death of Nathan Buchman, and was defeated for election in the Democratic presidential primary of 1938. At age 24, Senator Berry had been elected president of the International Printing Pressmen and Assistants' Union in 1907, a position he held until his death in 1948.

[43] Statement of James Francis O'Connor, Representative from Montana, March 21, 1941, during congressional debate over the 1941 Fifth Supplemental National Defense Act (see *Congressional Record*, vol. 87, part 15. 77th Congress, 1st Session, p. 2564.)

[44] The Buy American Act (41 U.S.C. §§10a through 10d, as amended), enacted in 1933, is the major domestic source restriction governing procurement by all of the federal government. It restricts U.S. government procurement by giving preference to domestically produced, manufactured, or home-grown products. For further discussion of the Buy (continued...)

---

domestic labor by giving preference to domestically produced, manufactured, or home-grown products in government purchases, with certain exceptions. The Berry Amendment overrides many of these exceptions, primarily for food, clothing, and specialty metals.

The two major differences between the BAA and the Berry Amendment are that (1) the BAA applies only to federal government contracts to be carried out within the United States, while the Berry Amendment, which is for defense contracts only, is not limited to contracts within the United States; and (2) the BAA requires that "substantially all" of the costs of foreign components not exceed 50% of the cost of all components (thus, an item can be of 51% domestic content and still be in compliance with the BAA) while the Berry Amendment requires that items be 100% domestic in origin.

It should be noted that there are a number of other domestic source provisions which generally govern specific types of procurement; these provisions are not covered by the BAA or the Berry Amendment. These provisions will not be covered in this report but must be considered when determining whether or not a specific domestic source provision affects a particular type of procurement.[45]

What Is the Relevance of the Berry Amendment Today?

Some observers argue that the Berry Amendment restrictions may not always represent the best value to DOD or the federal government, nor is there always a justifiable national security interest to preserve certain items currently under the Berry Amendment. Nevertheless, others have asserted that U.S. workers and businesses have an expectation that Congress will consider their interests in determining procurement policies.

A number of Berry Amendment-restricted items may be in line with the original purpose and intent, based on the end use products that are produced. For example, certain items like chemical warfare protective clothing (composed of ballistic fibers, made from textiles) may warrant further study. Specialty metals may be critical and vital to the war-fighting effort if they are used for "high-tech" electronics and communications. Food restrictions, on the other hand, are not critical and may make it more difficult for DOD to take advantage of commercial business practices. In an increasingly globalized economy, many food suppliers find it difficult to adhere to this restriction as it deviates from standard commercial business practices, so some may decline to sell to DOD. Many food suppliers who sell to DOD claim they are often forced to adopt unique, costly, and inefficient business practices to do business with the defense sector.[46]

(...continued)

American Act, refer to CRS Report 97-765, *The Buy American Act: Requiring Government Procurements to Come from Domestic Sources*, by John R. Luckey.

[45] See 41 U.S.C. §10a through 10d, and 10 U.S.C. §2533, Determinations of Public Interest under the Buy American Act. For further discussion of the Buy American Act, see CRS Report 97-765, *The Buy American Act: Requiring Government Procurements to Come from Domestic Sources*, by John R. Luckey. For further discussion of defense domestic source provisions not covered by the Buy American Act or the Berry Amendment, refer to Title 10 of the United States Code.

[46] According to Leslie G. Sarasin of the American Frozen Food Institute (AFFI), "The Berry Amendment required DOD to procure foods, entirely of U.S. origin ingredients. Often, DOD was forced to reject multi-ingredient, commercially available food items processed in the United States because the domestic origin of all ingredients and components of the product could not be demonstrated. This policy put DOD at odds with common commercial practice in the food industry, which typically follows U.S. tariff law in determining questions of foreign origin, and limited its access to the widest possible selection of products." Memorandum to the Defense Acquisition Regulations Council on AFFI comments on DOD's proposed interim rule regarding modification of the Berry Amendment, June 21, 2002. See (continued...)

Economic, social, and political factors come into play when examining the purpose and intent of the Berry Amendment. If the United States becomes dependent on purchasing equipment and supplies from foreign sources, what prevents an adversary from cutting off U.S. access to such items or refusing to build militarily critical items in times of crisis or conflict? Another argument for maintaining the Berry Amendment restrictions is that they often benefit small, minority-owned, and disadvantaged businesses, which may depend on DOD for their viability. According to congressional testimony, U.S. textile and apparel industries combined lost approximately 540,000 jobs during the 1990s.[47]

Some would argue that the Berry Amendment is still relevant today because of the tragic events of September 11, 2001. There are also concerns over the possibility of future acts of terrorism and the safety and security of the nation's food supply. Some specialty metals and steel products, items covered under the Berry Amendment, are produced by distressed U.S. industries. One such company, Bethlehem Steel, one of the largest U.S. steel manufacturers, filed for Chapter 11 bankruptcy protection, in part because of the competition from cheaper, foreign-made, and possibly subsidized steel.[48] Additionally, the procurement of certain items like ballistic fibers (found in body armor, which is critical to the protection of U.S. military troops) is restricted to domestic producers under the Berry Amendment. Generally, proponents of the Berry Amendment have argued that these types of restrictions are necessary to maintain a viable industrial base, and that the Berry Amendment serves as some protection for critical industries by keeping them healthy and viable in times of peace and war. For these reasons, some believe that this is not the time to change the provisions of the Berry Amendment, arguing that the United States should maintain its current capacity, at a minimum, to feed and clothe its military forces.

However, critics argue that the Berry Amendment can undercut free market competition and may produce other negative effects, such as reducing business incentives to modernize, causing inefficiency in some industries due to a lack of competition, and causing higher costs to DOD (because the military services may pay more for "protected" products than the market requires). Critics also contend that the Berry Amendment promotes U.S. trade policies that might undermine international trade agreements. For example, the delays associated with the procurement of body armor for U.S. troops in Iraq were a source of congressional criticism including during the 108th Congress.[49]

(...continued)

DFARS Case 2002-D002, at http://www.affi.com/policy.asp.

[47] Statement of Evan Joffe, Marketing Manager of Springfield, LLC, before the House Committee on Small Business, May 22, 2001.

[48] Behr, Peter. Bethlehem Steel Files for Bankruptcy; Struggles with Competition from Imports, Labor Costs Exacerbated by Aftermath of Attacks. *Washington Post*, October 16, 2001, p. E01. Bethlehem Steel, a 97-year-old company based in Bethlehem, PA, was the 25th steel company to file for bankruptcy protection since 1998. The company listed $4.3 billion in assets, $6.75 billion in liabilities, including an unfunded health care obligation of $1.85 billion.

[49] According to Vice Admiral Keith W. Lippert, United States Navy, who is the Director of the Defense Logistics Agency, the Army has adequately equipped all of the U.S. troops with the Interceptor Body Armor. In his testimony on March 30, 2004, before the House Armed Services Subcommittee on Readiness, he reported that "As we prepared (for Operation Iraqi Freedom), we built on lessons learned from previous conflicts. Our preparations were good in some areas, but needed to improve in others. I've discussed our joint planning with the Services in advance of the operation. In some cases, actual demand for items exceeded projections. For example, the Small Arms Protective Inserts—the SAPI plates you've all heard about—the estimated FY2003 requirements were seventeen million dollars. For a very good reason, the protection of our American war fighter—The Army increased their requirement for Interceptor Body Armor. Today all troops in Iraq are equipped with Interceptor Body Armor. To meet the increased requirement, funded requisitions began coming to us in January 2003. By November 2003, we actually bought three hundred seventy (continued...)

Application of the Berry Amendment

Department of Defense Views of the Berry Amendment

DOD officials have expressed contrasting views about the necessity for the Berry Amendment. Then Secretary of Defense Richard Cheney[50] issued a 1989 report to Congress called *The Impact of Buy American Restrictions Affecting Defense Procurement*. The report suggested that an alternative to the Berry Amendment would be a specifically targeted approach to provide DOD with the ability to establish assured sources of supply for mobilization purposes through existing mobilization base planning under the Defense Production Act.[51] The report concluded that "statutory and regulatory policies and other federal and DOD acquisition regulations like the Berry Amendment, which prohibit or impede foreign-source participation in U.S. defense contracting, constitute a considerable departure from the concept of full and open competition."

In 1997, the DOD Acquisition Reform Executive Focus Group's final report called for the elimination of some Berry Amendment restrictions on food, clothing, and textiles, while retaining restrictions on specialty metals and measuring tools.

A former DLA Deputy Director, Major General (Ret.) Charles R. Henry, testified that the Berry Amendment was critical to the maintenance of a "warm" U.S. industrial base during periods of adversity and war. He summed up his opinion, as follows:

> The point here is that, through the Berry Amendment, our defense procurement establishment is able to maintain a stable of independent, competing producers who understand the mil-specs of different items and who have the commitment to service the U.S. military. They are there for our military when there is a surge in requirements—as there was with Desert Storm—and they must be there during peacetime.[52]

Other Views

Some proponents of the Berry Amendment believe that the U.S. military should not be dependent on foreign sources for critical textile products and that dependency on foreign sources for military items could lead to problems with supply, demand, delays, and a potentially adversarial relationship with suppliers during times of war or military mobilization. Furthermore, some believe that the Berry Amendment should be expanded to include other important industries and those new federal agencies like the Department of Homeland Security should be covered by the provisions of the Berry Amendment.[53] However, some representatives of domestic and foreign

---

(...continued)

million dollars of the SAPI plates - using exigency contracts, awarded within thirty days, with an average delivery beginning within eighty-three days. The Army Audit Agency conducted a special inspection of body armor and found that we were timely in making awards and that quality products were delivered on time. However, SAPI production right now is constrained by the availability of raw materials, mainly the ceramic tiles contained in the plates. At present, known worldwide production of qualified ballistic packages is limited to twenty-five thousand SAPI sets (or fifty thousand plates) per month."

[50] Secretary of Defense, March 1989 - January 1993.

[51] For further discussion on the Defense Production Act, see nondistributable CRS Report RS20587, *Defense Production Act: Purpose and Scope*, by Daniel H. Else, available from author.

[52] Testimony before the Oversight and Investigations Subcommittee, House Committee on Education and the Workforce. Hearing on Federal Prison Industries' Proposed Military Clothing Production Expansion - Assessing Existing Protections for Workers, Business, and FPI's Federal Agency Customers. October 5, 2000.

[53] It should be noted that H.R. 1 (111th Congress), the American Recovery and Reinvestment Act of 2009 (P.L. 111-5) (continued...)

---

companies have criticized the Berry Amendment, stating that it undercuts free market competition, may promote discriminatory practices, robs businesses of incentives to modernize, causes inefficiency in some industries due to a lack of competition, and results in higher costs to DOD, because the military services pay more for "protected" products than the market requires. Some critics of the Berry Amendment also argue that the United States will lose its technological edge in the absence of competition and alienate foreign trading partners, thereby provoking retaliations and loss of foreign sales. They assert that the Berry Amendment will ultimately reduce the ability of the United States to negotiate and persuade its allies to sell or not sell to developing countries. They contend that the Berry Amendment promotes U.S. trade policies that undermine the international trade agreements. Furthermore, restrictions on food mean that in most cases it is illegal for DOD to purchase an item or food if it is a foreign item or if it has any foreign ingredient or processing. On the other hand, critics have also expressed concern over the increased levels of imported, ready to wear goods, and the prevalent "sweat shop conditions" of foreign markets.

In 2006, the Berry Amendment Reform Coalition (a group of associations and member companies that support legislative reforms to the Berry Amendment) proposed legislative reforms that advocated for exceptions to the Berry Amendment for domestic specialty metals.[54] The passage of the John Warner National Defense Authorization Act for FY2007 (P.L. 109-364, Sections 842 and 843) effectively moved the specialty metal provision out of the Berry Amendment and into a separate section of Title 10. The specialty metals clause provides protection for strategic materials critical to national security.

Options for Congress

The Army's black beret controversy, which revealed that the berets are not 100% domestic in origin, and the resulting waiver of Berry Amendment restrictions to allow DLA to procure the berets from foreign sources raised questions which have not been settled, as to the original purpose, intent, and value of the Berry Amendment. Congress may choose to examine the domestic source restrictions under the Berry Amendment and other procurement provisions and to determine whether they help or hurt the defense industrial base, including relationships with foreign trading partners.

Option 1: Take No Action, Retain the Berry Amendment as Enacted

Congress may choose to take no action, to retain the current provisions of the Berry Amendment as enacted in law.

(...continued)

contained a provision (§604) which affected all funds appropriated or otherwise made available to DHS. These restrictions prohibited DHS from the purchase of certain textiles unless the items were grown, reprocessed, reused, or produced in the United States. §604 are sometimes referred to as the Kissell Amendment. Also, the Berry Amendment Extension Act was reintroduced by Representative Kissell on February 11, 2011, and referred to the House Homeland Security Subcommittee on Oversight, Investigations, and Management. The bill seeks to extend the provisions of the Berry Amendment to DHS.

[54] Berry Amendment Reform Coalition, https://oasis northgrum.com/general/docs/ BerryAmendmentReformCoalition.pdf.

Option 2: Eliminate Some Selected Restrictions

Congress might eliminate some selected restrictions, such as the restrictions on food. Eliminating the restrictions on purchasing food items (with less than 100% domestic content) would allow U.S. food suppliers to use more commercial business practices that are more cost effective. This move would arguably promote more competition and interest in selling food to DOD. For example, some in DOD believe that elimination of the food restriction would allow food suppliers greater and more practical latitude to use foreign ingredients and processing, in line with current commercial practice. Many food suppliers find this restriction to be the least practical and even trade associations of food suppliers have stated that this restriction makes it more difficult to do business with DOD. The Pentagon believes that the food provisions of the Buy American Act would continue to provide U.S. food suppliers a significant advantage over foreign suppliers.

Likewise, Congress could eliminate or modify the clothing restriction, allowing DOD to find the best item for the most competitive price.[55] DOD has reportedly known for 25 years that it does not produce a solely domestic beret.[56] One alternative would be for restricted items to be classified according to a prioritized system, with "high-tech" and "low-tech" classifications, which each could have different waiver requirements. Some military uniform components, such as the beret, could be classified as "low-tech," and therefore could be procured without a waiver. This option would most likely be opposed by groups such as the American Manufacturing Trade Action Coalition and the National Council of Textile Organizations.

Option 3: Adopt a "Componency Standard"

Congress might revise the Berry Amendment and amend the provisions to say that manufactured articles are considered domestic if "substantially all" of their components have been mined, produced, or manufactured domestically. This is similar to the requirements of the Buy American Act and could eliminate future procurement issues like those encountered in the Army black beret procurement.

Such a provision was proposed in the House-passed version of H.R. 1588, the FY2004 National Defense Authorization Act. Section 829, titled "Requirement Relating to Purchases by Department of Defense Subject to Buy American Act," would have broadened the definition of what makes an item "domestic" in origin. In Section 829, an item was defined as domestic and covered under the Buy American Act if it was at least 65% domestic in origin. Adoption of this provision would have provided DOD the authority to procure items that may be a combination of both domestic and foreign in origin. This provision alone would represent a significant departure from the 100% domestic requirement of the Berry Amendment, and more closely parallel the provisions of the BAA.[57] However, this provision was dropped in the final version of the bill.[58]

---

[55] However, the American Manufacturing Trade Action Coalition http://www.amtacdc.org advocates for the preservation of the Berry Amendment and the Buy American Act, so that the U.S. military does not become dependent on foreign sources for critical textile products.

[56] At the May 2, 2001, hearing before the House Committee on Small Business, Ms. Michele Goodman from Atlas Headwear, Inc. (a small business supplier based in Phoenix, Arizona) testified that American companies could have fulfilled the Army's black beret requirement had DLA's Defense Supply Center of Philadelphia been given enough time to proceed properly, and had the U.S. Army been more open minded about the type of beret it wanted. Her company attempted to bid for the beret contract, without success. See the prepared statement of Michele Goodman, "Black Beret Procurement: Business as Usual at the Pentagon?" House Committee on Small Business, May 2, 2001.

[57] The Buy American Act requires the federal government to procure items that are "substantially" composed of domestic materials, while the Berry Amendment requires that the Department of Defense procure items that are wholly (continued...)

Option 4: Study the Lessening or Elimination of Provisions

Congress could solicit the opinions of trade associations, labor organizations, and industry experts on the selected use of Berry Amendment restrictions and use of the waiver requirement. Many industry experts say that this approach is preferable to an "all or nothing" stance taken by some interest groups.

The American Apparel and Footwear Association (AAFA) supports the preservation of the Berry Amendment. AAFA believes that the controversy surrounding the procurement of the berets has helped shore up support for such a change in the law. The association has suggested that Congress might want to consider whether one particular restriction adversely impacts a U.S. company or its workers that might have become dependent upon the provisions of the Berry Amendment for their economic well-being.[59]

Option 5: Study What Percentage of Domestic Clothing, Textiles, Food, and Specialty Metals Is Sold to the Military

Congress might determine whether these markets are wholly dependent on the military or whether they represent a statistically significant portion of the total market. For example, during Desert Storm the apparel and textile industry proved that its surge capacity could rapidly respond to a major contingency and a sudden call-up for servicemen and women. The industry started with nine manufacturers producing 2 million camouflage fatigues in 1988; by 1991, the number of manufacturers increased to 16, producing some 5 million camouflage fatigues. Congress may also want to explore the impact of Berry Amendment restrictions on U.S. relationships with foreign trading partners.

Option 6: Appoint a "Berry Amendment Commission"

Congress might appoint a commission to study the effects of the Berry Amendment restrictions on the U.S. industrial base, national security, and the military's war-fighting capability. The commission could assess the economic, social, and political impact of current restrictions and make recommendations to the Congress. The commission could determine whether current coverage of the Berry Amendment is appropriate or whether it should be expanded or contracted.

Option 7: Audit and Investigate Berry Amendment Contracts

Congress could investigate all military procurement contracts for compliance with the Berry Amendment. Noting that congressional testimony suggested that DLA had known that the Bancroft Cap Company has used foreign suppliers for the past 25 years implies that there may be other similar instances that have been overlooked or underreported. Congress could direct the Government Accountability Office[60] or the DOD Inspector General to conduct an audit of a representative sample of contracts awarded for each restricted item under the Berry Amendment, including whether end products incorporated materials from foreign sources.

(...continued)

(100%) domestic.

[58] H.R. 1588, the National Defense Authorization Act for 2004, was enacted as P.L. 108-136 on November 24, 2003.

[59] AAFA Legislative Update, March/April/May 2001.

[60] Effective July 7, 2004, the General Accounting Office's legal name is the Government Accountability Office.

Legislative Activity

Several domestic source provisions concerning the Berry Amendment were introduced during the 110th-113th Congresses. Some were proposed, others enacted into law. One common theme was the broadening of the Secretary of Defense's waiver authority (authority to waive the Berry Amendment) when the Secretary believed that there was an unusual and compelling reason to procure items from foreign sources. Other provisions sought to broaden the provisions of the Berry Amendment to cover new items not currently covered (like athletic footwear) or additional agencies (like the Department of Homeland Security).

113th Congress

Legislation Proposed

- On September 30, 2013, DOD issued an interim rule which would amend the Defense Federal Acquisition Regulation Supplement (DFARS) to implement provisions of H.R. 4310 (P.L. 112-239), the National Defense Authorization Act of 2013, that require compliance with the Berry Amendment. Section 826 of H.R. 4310 requires that textiles procured by DOD for the production of military uniforms for the Afghan National Army or the Afghan National Police must be in compliance with the Berry Amendment. Related to Section 826, Section 842 amends Section 886 of H.R. 4986 (P.L. 110-181) to reflect the authority to acquire products and services from Iraq and Afghanistan.[61]

- On May 23, 2013, two bills were introduced with similar purposes. S. 1051 was introduced in the Senate while H.R. 2188 was introduced in the House. Both bills would amend Title 37, U.S.C. to ensure that footwear furnished or obtained by allowance for enlisted members of the Armed Forces upon their initial entry would meet the requirements of the Berry Amendment. The two bills would require DOD to comply with the Berry Amendment by purchasing athletic footwear in the same way as other military uniform purchases. Currently, enlisted members receive a stipend through vouchers to buy athletic footwear, and there is no requirement that the footwear be domestic in origin.

- S. 2114, the Berry Amendment Extension Act, was introduced on February 15, 2011, and referred to the Senate Committee on Homeland Security and Government Affairs. H.R. 679, a similar bill, was introduced on February 11, 2011, and was referred to the House Homeland Security Subcommittee on Oversight, Investigations, and Management. Similar bills have been introduced in previous Congresses.

- H.R. 2955, the "American Shoes for American Service Members Act," was introduced on September 15, 2011, and referred to the House Armed Services Committee. This provision would amend Title 10 U.S.C. Section 2533a (b) (1) (B) by clarifying that the Berry Amendment includes athletic footwear as well as the materials and components of the footwear.

---

[61] Defense Federal Acquisition Regulation Supplement: Acquisitions in Support of Operations in Afghanistan (DFARS Case 2013-D009). Interim rule, September 30, 2013. Comments on the interim rule will be accepted through November 29, 2013. Accessed online at https://www.federalregister.gov/articles/2013/09/30/2013-23743/defense-federal-acquisition-regulation-supplement-acquisitions-in-support-of-operations-in#h-9.

112th Congress

Legislation Enacted

P.L. 112-81, the National Defense Authorization Act for FY2012 (H.R. 1540) contained a provision (§821) which clarified the intent of the Berry Amendment when applied to the purchase of tents, tarpaulins, or covers from domestic sources.[62]

P.L. 112-81 also contained a provision (§822) which repealed the sunset of the authority to procure fire resistant rayon fiber, from foreign sources, used for the production of uniforms.

Legislation Proposed

S. 2114, the Berry Amendment Extension Act, was introduced on February 15, 2012, by Senator John D. Rockefeller and referred to the Senate Committee on Homeland Security and Government Affairs. H.R. 679, a similar bill, was introduced by Representative Larry Kissell on February 11, 2011, and referred to the House Homeland Security Subcommittee on Oversight, Investigations, and Management. Both bills seek to extend the provisions of the Berry Amendment to the Department of Homeland Security. Similar bills have been introduced in previous Congresses.

H.R. 2955, the "American Shoes for American Servicemembers Act," was introduced on September 15, 2011, by Representative Mike Michaud. This provision would amend Title 10 U.S.C. Section 2533a (b) (1) (B) by clarifying that the Berry Amendment includes athletic footwear as well as the materials and components of the footwear. The bill was referred to the House Armed Services Committee.

111th Congress

Legislation Proposed

H.R. 6262, the Jobs through Procurement Act, was introduced on September 29, 2010, by then-Representative Phil Hare. The proposed bill sought to strengthen the domestic sourcing requirements of the Berry Amendment and the Buy American Act. The bill was referred to the Committees for House Oversight and Government Reform and the House Armed Services Committee.

H.R. 5013, the Implementing Management for Performance and Related Reforms to Obtain Value in Every Acquisition Act of 2010, was introduced on April 14, 2010, by Representative Robert Andrews and referred to the Senate Armed Services Committee. The proposed measure would have contained a provision (§409) that expressed a "sense of Congress" that

> in order to create jobs, level the playing field for domestic manufacturers, and strengthen economic recovery, it is the sense of Congress that the Department of Defense should—
>
> (1) Ensure full contractor and subcontractor compliance with the Berry Amendment (10 U.S.C. 2533a) and the Buy American Act (41 U.S.C. 10a et seq.); and
>
> (2) Not procure products made by manufacturers in the United States that violate labor standards as defined under the laws of the United States.[63]

---

[62] §2533a (b) (1) (C) of Title 10, U.S.C., is amended by inserting "and the structural components thereof" after the word "tents."

H.R. 5013 also included two amendments (H.Amdt. 615 and H.Amdt. 617) that propose to strengthen the application of the Berry Amendment to defense procurement. H.Amdt. 615 would have required GAO to conduct a study of certain procurement items to determine if there is sufficient domestic production to adequately supply the Armed Forces, and to evaluate whether such items could be made in the United States under the Berry Amendment. H.Amdt. 617 would have expressed the sense of Congress that DOD should operate in full compliance through the acquisition process of the Berry Amendment and the Buy American Act, and that DOD should not procure products made by manufacturers in the United States that violate U.S. labor standards.

H.R. 3116, the Berry Amendment Extension Act, was introduced on July 7, 2009, by Representative Larry Kissell. The proposed measure would have prohibited the purchase of clothing, tents, tarpaulins, and certain other textiles unless the items are grown, reprocessed, reused, or produced in the United States. The bill was referred to the Senate Homeland Security and Governmental Affairs Committee. No further action was taken.

110th Congress

Legislation Proposed

H.R. 917, the Berry Amendment Extension Act, was introduced on February 8, 2007, by Representative Robin Hayes. The proposed measure would have prohibited DHS from the purchase of clothing, tents, tarpaulins, and certain other textiles unless the items are grown, reprocessed, reused, or produced in the United States. The bill was referred to the House Homeland Security Subcommittee on Management, Investigations, and Oversight. No further action was taken.

Author Contact Information

Valerie Bailey Grasso
Specialist in Defense Acquisition
vgrasso@crs.loc.gov, 7-7617

(...continued)

[63] §409, Sense of the Congress in Regard to Compliance with the Berry Amendment, the Buy American Act, and Labor Standards of the United States.